FIRST PEOPLES

APACHE

VALERIE BODDEN

CREATIVE EDUCATION ✦ CREATIVE PAPERBACKS

Published by Creative Education and Creative Paperbacks
P.O. Box 227, Mankato, Minnesota 56002
Creative Education and Creative Paperbacks are imprints of
The Creative Company
www.thecreativecompany.us

Design and production by Christine Vanderbeek
Art direction by Rita Marshall
Printed in the United States of America

Photographs by Alamy (Angela Hampton Picture Library,
Anders Ryman), Bridgeman Images (Apache Chief James A
Garfield, American Photographer, [20th century]/Private
Collection/© Look and Learn/Elgar Collection; Nar-Ah-Kig-
Gee-Ah Tzur [Kit Carson's Apache Scout], c.1900–10 [oil
on canvas], Phillips, Bert Geer [1868–1956]/Fred Jones Jr.
Museum of Art, University of Oklahoma, USA/Given in
memory of Roxanne P. Thams by William Thams, 2003),
Corbis (Corbis, Tom Till/SuperStock), Shutterstock (Zack
Frank, Kresimir IV, Miloje, Emre Tarimcioglu, vectorbest,
Edward Westmacott), SuperStock (SuperStock)

Library of Congress Cataloging-in-Publication data
Names: Bodden, Valerie, author.
Title: Apache / Valerie Bodden.
Series: First Peoples.
Includes bibliographical references and index.
Summary: An introduction to the Apache lifestyle and
history, including their forced relocation and how they keep
traditions alive today. An Apache story recounts how the
mountains were formed.
Identifiers:
ISBN 978-1-60818-901-4 (hardcover)
ISBN 978-1-62832-517-1 (pbk)
ISBN 978-1-56660-953-1 (eBook)
This title has been submitted for CIP processing under
LCCN 2017940103.

CCSS: RI.1.1, 2, 3, 4, 5, 6, 7; RI.2.1, 2, 3, 4, 5, 6; RI.3.1, 2, 3, 5;
RF.1.1, 3, 4; RF.2.3, 4

First Edition HC   9 8 7 6 5 4 3 2 1
First Edition PBK   9 8 7 6 5 4 3 2 1

TABLE *of* CONTENTS

SOUTHWESTERN PEOPLE

The Apache lived in the American Southwest. The word *Apache* probably came from the Zuni Indians. It meant "enemy." The Apache called themselves *Ndee*. This meant "The People."

 Some Apache were based in the Chisos Mountains of West Texas in the 1700s.

There were six Apache tribes, or groups. They spoke in similar ways. Some tribes shared TRADITIONS. But they lived in different parts of the Southwest.

A famous leader called Geronimo (at center) belonged to the Chiricahua Apache group.

APACHE LIFE

Many Apache lived in dome-shaped homes. They used sticks, brush, and grass to build them. Other Apache lived in cone-shaped tepees.

 The rounded form of an Apache home is known as a wickiup in the American Southwest.

The members of an Apache family lived close to each other. Families in an area formed a local group. A chief led the group.

 Chiefs like James A. Garfield (left), led warriors to protect their families and land.

Apache women planted crops. They picked wild plants like MESCAL to eat. They made clothes. They wove baskets. Apache men hunted deer, elk, and bison. They fought in wars. They went on raids to steal horses.

 The Apache traveled to hunt big game animals like bison, which lived on the plains.

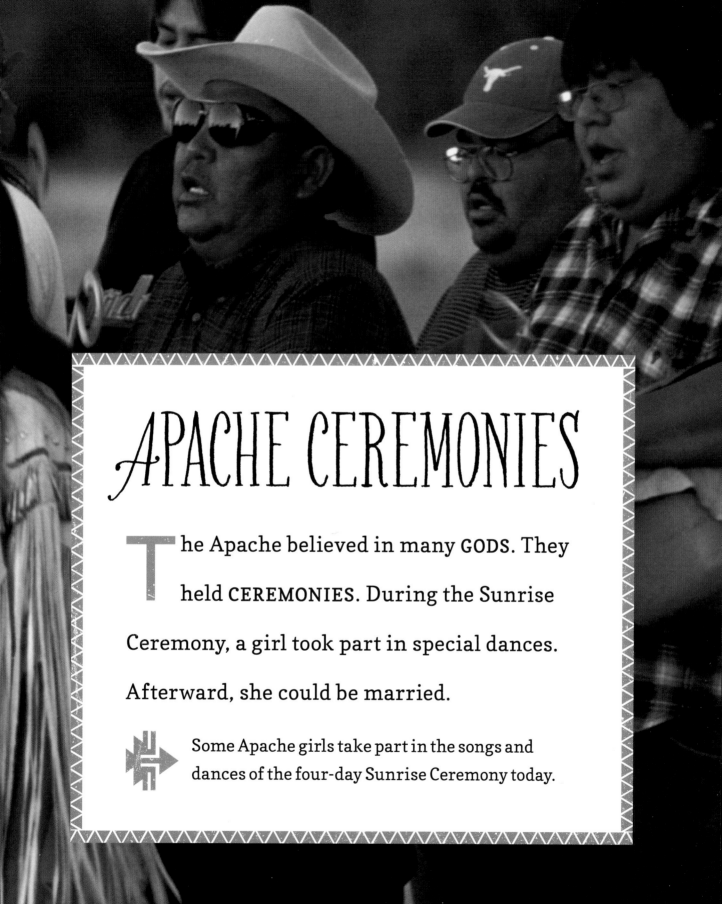

APACHE CEREMONIES

The Apache believed in many GODS. They held CEREMONIES. During the Sunrise Ceremony, a girl took part in special dances. Afterward, she could be married.

Some Apache girls take part in the songs and dances of the four-day Sunrise Ceremony today.

HORSES AND RESERVATIONS

The Apache were some of the first American Indians to ride horses. They stole horses from Spanish SETTLERS. The Spanish took Apache children to sell as slaves.

 Horses helped the Apache and other peoples hunt bigger animals and travel farther.

In the 1870s, the government made the Apache move to reservations. These were areas of land set aside for American Indians. The Apache had to cut their hair. They had to wear American-style clothing.

 Children from reservations were often sent to schools far away from their parents.

BEING APACHE

Today, many Apache still live on reservations in New Mexico and Arizona. Some hold the Sunrise Ceremony. Many women make baskets. They keep their traditions alive.

 Special clothing is made and worn for ceremonies and other big events.

AN APACHE STORY

During the long winters, the Apache told stories to explain the world. In one story, a giant elk ate people. A child of the sun wanted to save the people. He shot four arrows into Elk's heart. Then he ran away through a tunnel. Elk followed. His antlers dug into the ground. They threw up huge chunks of soil. These became the mountains.

GLOSSARY

CEREMONIES ⟶ special acts carried out according to set rules

GODS ⟶ beings that people believe have special powers and control the world

MESCAL ⟶ a small cactus that does not have spines

SETTLERS ⟶ people who come to live in a new area

TRADITIONS ⟶ beliefs, stories, or ways of doing things that are passed down from parents to their children

READ MORE

Fullman, Joe. *Native North Americans: Dress, Eat, Write, and Play Just Like the Native Americans*. Mankato, Minn.: QEB, 2010.

Morris, Ting. *Arts and Crafts of the Native Americans*. North Mankato, Minn.: Smart Apple Media, 2007.

WEBSITES

Apache Indian Photo Gallery
http://www.impurplehawk.com/apgallery.html
Check out historical photos of the Apache.

Wickiups: Sturdy but Temporary Structures
http://www.texasbeyondhistory.net/kids/houses/wickiups.html
Learn more about how Apache homes were built.

Note: Every effort has been made to ensure that the websites listed above are suitable for children, that they have educational value, and that they contain no inappropriate material. However, because of the nature of the Internet, it is impossible to guarantee that these sites will remain active indefinitely or that their contents will not be altered.

INDEX